THE JEWISH WORLD

Douglas Charing

Macdonald

Editor
Belinda Hollyer
Design
Richard Johnson
Picture Research
Caroline Mitchell
Production
Rosemary Bishop

Consultant
Rabbi Sybil Sheridan
Ealing Liberal Synagogue
London

A MACDONALD BOOK

©Macdonald & Co (Publishers) 1983
First published in Great Britain in 1983
by Macdonald & Co (Publishers) Ltd
London & Sydney
A BPCC plc company

Reprinted in 1985
ISBN 0 356 07522 2

Made and printed by
Henri Proost, Belgium

Macdonald & Co (Publishers) Ltd
Maxwell House
74 Worship Street
London EC2A 2EN

Cover picture: A Jewish family celebrating the festival of *Succot* in their home-made *succah* booth.

Endpapers: A *Succot* service in a synagogue. The adults are holding palm branches and citron fruit. The children are waving willow and myrtle leaves.

Title page: A group of Jewish children with their teacher, at the Western Wall in Jerusalem. The Wall is all that remains of the ancient second Temple.

Contents page: A Jew praying at the Western Wall.

Contents

8 **Who are the Jews?**

10 **Jewish beginnings**

12 **The sad centuries**

14 **A world religion**

16 **The basic beliefs**

18 **Judaism's many faces**

20 **The synagogue**

22 **A window to heaven**

24 **The sacred books**

26 **Signs and symbols**

28 **Growing up Jewish**

30 **The adult years**

32 **A day of delight**

34 **Celebrations**

36 **Days of joy**

38 **Dreaming of Zion**

40 **The Jewish connection**

42 **A glossary of useful words**

43 **The Jewish calendar**

44 **Books for further reading**

44 **Places to visit**

44 **Helpful organisations**

45 **Index**

A note about spelling

Hebrew has its own alphabet, and the English versions of Hebrew words can be spelled in several different ways. You may see, for example, the word *Hanukah* spelled *Chanukah*, or *Chanuka*, or *Channukah*. In this book we have chosen spellings which are the closest match between the original Hebrew sounds and English sounds.

Sometimes the spelling also shows how the Hebrew words are formed. *Rosh ha-Shanah*, for example, the name of the Jewish New Year, has been written like that because '*Shanah*' is the word for 'Year', and '*ha*' is the word for 'the'.

Who are the Jews?

There is really no single or easy answer to the question 'who are the Jews?'. Jewish people can trace their history back for thousands of years, and they have lived all over the world. In early times they were known as the Israelites (from their ancestor Jacob, who was also called Israel), or as the Hebrews (from the name of a nomadic people, of which they were part). Later these names were also linked to a country, and a language. But today people from hundreds of countries, speaking as many languages, are all Jews. What binds them together?

A religious group

Religion is obviously a central point for describing Jews. Anyone who believes in the Jewish God, follows Jewish traditions and obeys the religious laws can become a Jew.

But someone whose mother was Jewish is also considered to be Jewish themselves. This means that even those who are not necessarily religious are included as Jews.

A Jewish race

Since the 19th century, many people have talked about a Jewish race. But the idea of a race of Jews is wrong, for there is really only one race of people in the world—the human race! The first Jews were certainly part of the semitic group of peoples, but this group includes many other peoples as well—the Arabs, for example.

A Jewish nation

There was a Jewish nation in ancient times, but this title is no longer accurate. Not even the state of Israel can be called a Jewish nation, for not all of its citizens are Jews. Israel is really the Israeli nation, rather than the Jewish nation. In any case, most of the world's Jews live outside the state of Israel. They are citizens of the countries in which they live, not Israeli citizens.

A people

Perhaps the best and most useful way of describing Jews is to call them a people. This can include those who are firm believers in the Jewish religion, and those who support the progress of Israel as a Jewish homeland. It also includes those Jews who are not religious and do not support Israel, but who are very aware of their Jewish roots.

Left: A Jewish family, whose original home was in Iran, celebrate the Passover in Jerusalem.

Left: These Jewish women belong to a synagogue in Cochin, India. Their clothes reflect their country's culture, while their surroundings reflect their religion.

Jewish beginnings

Leaders of Judaism
Although Moses is the most important of these, Judaism has no single founder, unlike many of the other religions of the world. Throughout its long history the Jewish religion has had many leaders and prophets, whose ideas have been moulded into a single pattern. They all lived thousands of years ago, during the time of such great empires as Egypt, Babylon and Rome. The empires have long since crumbled, but the religion continues to flourish.

Abraham
Abraham is the first of three men who are called the 'patriarchs', or fathers, of Judaism. The other two are his son Isaac, and his grandson Jacob.

Abraham is not only an important person for Jews but also for Christians and Muslims —in fact, he is the father of all three religions. For the Jews, Abraham is the father of 'monotheism', which means 'faith in one God'. He, it is believed, was the first to teach that there is only one God, who created the world, and that only God should be worshipped.

Moses
Centuries after Abraham another leader emerged, called Moses. He had the task of leading the Jewish people out of Egypt and into the promised land of Israel. It was through Moses that God gave the first five books of the Bible to the Jewish people. According to Jewish tradition these books are known as the Five Books of Moses, or the *Torah*. Moses is also regarded as the most important prophet, and a great teacher.

There is an interesting story about the calling of Moses by God. Moses was working as a shepherd when he noticed that a newly-born lamb was missing from the flock. He began to search, and hours later found the lamb, tired, cold and frightened. Moses took hold of the creature gently, comforted it and gave it food, and wrapped it in his cloak. God saw that such a man, who went out of his way to help a small animal, would be a good shepherd for God's people.

Ezra
One of the worst times in Jewish history was when the Babylonians invaded Israel, destroyed Jerusalem and the Temple, and

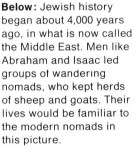

Below: Jewish history began about 4,000 years ago, in what is now called the Middle East. Men like Abraham and Isaac led groups of wandering nomads, who kept herds of sheep and goats. Their lives would be familiar to the modern nomads in this picture.

took away the Jewish leaders as captives. Nearly fifty years later·some of the captives returned, and a man called Ezra became their leader.

Ezra inspired the people to rebuild their Temple. He also introduced many reforms, which made sure that Judaism would survive —even if the Temple was again destroyed, and the Jewish people exiled once more.

Hillel and Akiva

Two people from later Jewish writings are particularly famous—and the first, called Hillel, lived almost two thousand years ago. He was such an important leader that the interpretation of many Jewish laws follows his examples. Hillel was once asked to explain the essence of his religion, and he replied: "Do not do unto others what you would not have others do unto you."

Akiva lived just after Hillel. He was the most talented, original and influential man of his generation, yet he could not read or write until he reached the age of forty. One of his many sayings is: "Beloved is man, for he was created in the image of God." Akiva was burned to death by the Romans.

Left: The teachings of Moses form the central part of Jewish belief. In this old Italian painting, Moses is shown holding the stone tablets he received from God. The first words of the Ten Commandments are shown on the tablets, written in Hebrew—but the artist didn't get the Hebrew exactly right!

Left: A reconstructed model of the second Temple. The actual Temple was built in Jerusalem, almost 2,500 years ago. It replaced the first Temple, built by Solomon 1,000 years earlier and later destroyed.

The sad centuries

The loss of their land

Nineteen centuries ago the land of Israel was occupied and ruled by the Romans. At first the Romans allowed the Jews religious freedom, but later they tried to crush Jewish power and influence. In the end they destroyed the Jewish Temple, and stopped Jews from living in—or even entering—Jerusalem. They also outlawed Jewish education, and killed any Jews who tried to continue teaching. Many Jews fled into a second exile from their homeland.

New lands, old troubles

In the centuries which followed, groups of Jews settled in many different countries. But they were often mistrusted by their new neighbours, and the mistrust frequently turned into hatred and persecution.

Jews had only two things left from their rich history: their God, and their customs. These were not just important in religious ways; they were also essential for pride and survival. But to other people such differences were dangerous and threatening. Jewish customs were misunderstood, or used as false evidence against the Jews.

Christian countries were often the worst places for Jews to live, and many Jews were massacred there. Sometimes the whole Jewish population of a town was killed, and their property confiscated. And, as a final weapon against the rest, there was always expulsion: from England, for example, in 1290, and from parts of France in 1306.

The Inquisition

Jews in Muslim Spain prospered for many centuries, and the peaceful atmosphere produced an outstanding generation of writers and thinkers. But this was followed by a time of intolerance and oppression under Muslim rulers, and under the Christian rulers who later replaced them.

In 1492 the Spanish Jews were given a choice: to convert to Christianity, or to leave Spain. Thousands left, but some Jews remained and pretended to convert. When the authorities discovered that, they set up special courts called the Inquisition. They thought the Jews could be persuaded that their beliefs were wrong. When words did not work the Inquisition used torture and death instead.

The Nazi nightmare

In this century, European Jews became the major victims of another persecution. It took only a few years—from 1937 to 1945—for the Nazis to kill six million Jews. Terrible concentration camps were set up, where people were shot, gassed and burned, and others died from starvation and disease. Thousands of non-Jews shared this fate.

One million Jewish children were among the victims, and the name of one girl has become a modern legend around the world. Anne Frank was only 16 when she died. She wrote in her now famous diary: "In spite of everything, I still believe that people are good at heart."

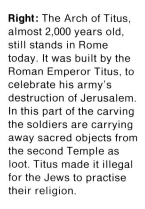

Right: The Arch of Titus, almost 2,000 years old, still stands in Rome today. It was built by the Roman Emperor Titus, to celebrate his army's destruction of Jerusalem. In this part of the carving the soldiers are carrying away sacred objects from the second Temple as loot. Titus made it illegal for the Jews to practise their religion.

Far left: In the Middle Ages many Jews were made to wear special clothes. These pointed hats were one way of setting Jews apart from other people, and making them look ridiculous.

Left: Eastern European Jews have led sad and difficult lives for centuries. This picture shows a Russian family in the 19th century, who are being forced to move from their home.

Left: The Germans occupied Poland in World War II. This group of Jewish women and children in Warsaw is being rounded-up at gun point by Nazi soldiers.

A world religion

Jews have been great travellers throughout history—sometimes as traders, sometimes as refugees. Over the centuries they made contact with most parts of the world, and the various groups of Jews today owe their differences to these early settlements.

The major groups

There are two main groups in world Jewry: the Ashkenasim, and the Sephardim. The word 'Ashkenasim' comes from the Hebrew word for Germany, and describes the Jews who lived in France and Germany, and who fled from persecution to Poland, Russia and parts of central Europe. Before 1933 they made up 90% of the world's Jews, but now the figure is nearer 80%.

The word 'Sephardim' comes from the Hebrew word for Spain, and describes the Jews from Spain and Portugal who fled to north Africa, Greece and Italy. Jews from the Yemen, and from some other Asian countries, are often called orientals, but they are usually included with the Sephardic Jews, with whom they have much in common.

Differences

The differences between the Ashkenasim and the Sephardim are not in belief or teachings. They are differences in the arrangement of prayers, the method of pronouncing Hebrew, the choice of melodies and chants for public worship, and the way in which some customs are carried out.

Both groups also developed their own everyday languages. The Ashkenasim used a language called Yiddish, which is a mixture of Hebrew and medieval German. The Sephardim used a language called Ladino; a mixture of Hebrew and medieval Spanish. Both languages are written with Hebrew letters, although Yiddish may also be written in the Russian alphabet. While some people continue to speak Yiddish, Ladino speakers are now very rare indeed.

Life styles

In general, the Ashkenasim lived in Christian countries while the Sephardim lived in Muslim countries. During the Middle Ages Sephardi Jews lived busy lives, on more or less equal terms with their Muslim neighbours. Many of them became important diplomats, doctors, architects and scholars, and studied Arabic as well as Jewish learning.

The European Ashkenasim had a much harder time. They were kept apart from other people, and forbidden any occupation except for money lending. So they concentrated all their energies on Jewish learning. In recent times, however, the Ashkenasim have led much freer lives. Now they work in many different fields, including science, medicine and the arts.

Other groups

Some other Jewish communities retain their own customs. The Falashas of Ethiopia have their own language, called *Be'ez*, and even use it to write their *Torah* scrolls. The *B'nei Israel* community in India have a special festival for the prophet Elijah. This celebrates a tradition that Elijah once appeared in India, and ascended into heaven from there.

Right: These graphs show the major centres of Jewish population in 1982. There are about 14½ million Jews in the world now, which represents less than ½% of the world's population.

Most Jews today, as in ancient times, do not live in Israel. More Jews live in the state of New York, in the USA, than in the cities of Jerusalem, Tel Aviv and Haifa combined!

World population of Jews

- Israel 23%
- USSR 14%
- Europe 10%
- Rest of world 8.6%
- South America 3.4%
- North America 41%

City population comparisons

1,998,000	New York
455,000	Los Angeles
380,000	Paris
335,000	Tel Aviv
298,000	Jerusalem
285,000	Moscow
250,000	Buenos Aires

Left: Sephardi *Torah* scrolls are kept inside special containers, which open at the front to display the scrolls. This container is made from wood, but many are made from precious metals, and decorated with rich carvings.

This scroll, in a Tunisian synagogue, is more than 1,500 years old. The silver plates that surround the Ark have been donated by members of the local Jewish community.

Below: Ashkenasi Jews wrap their *Torah* scrolls in embroidered cloths. When the cloths are removed, the scrolls can be wound from one roller to the other as they are read.

Fully-dressed scrolls are often decorated with breastplates and silver bells on top of the cloths.

The basic beliefs

God

The Jewish belief about God is simple. There is only one God, and he alone is prayed to. He is the creator of the universe, but he is also near to every creature, and listens to their prayers.

Although there is only one God, the Jewish religion has many names for God. God's real name is so holy that it is never mentioned—and its pronunciation is unknown. Other names are used instead, such as God, Lord, Father, or a phrase which means 'the Holy One, blessed be he'.

Good and evil

Judaism teaches that because God is good, so people should be good. The Jewish religion demands that Jews should love both God and all people. However, since God has given humans the ability to choose what they do, there will be times when people do bad, even evil, things. Judaism is aware that everyone has an inclination to do evil, as well as one to do good. But God will always forgive sins as long as people are truly sorry, and show that they will try to put things right. Repentance, prayer and good deeds will make up for evil ways.

A chosen people

An important Jewish teaching is the special relationship that exists between God and the Jewish people. Since God chose the Jews by giving them his laws, the Jews regard themselves as his chosen people.

But this does not mean that other nations and peoples are in any way inferior. It means that Jews have special duties and obligations to perform, and only by remaining faithful to their religion can they continue to claim this relationship.

The Jews see themselves as a 'light to the nations', which means teaching the world about God and his laws. But it does not mean that Jews want everyone to become Jewish—and although many people do convert to Judaism, it is not a religion that seeks converts. Muslims and Christians already share the same view of God, and Judaism simply asks that all people, whatever their beliefs, should live their lives with love, respect and care for other people. It recognises that there are important values in all faiths—and an ancient Jewish teaching says that the good of all nations and religions have a share in God's future kingdom.

The Messiah

Another important teaching is concerned with a future event. Our world today is scarred, as it has always been, by wars and conflict. The Jewish hope is one of future peace and harmony, and Judaism's sacred books speak of a leader sent by God to bring peace to mankind. He is called the Messiah, or the Anointed One. Many have claimed to be the Messiah over the centuries, but Jews believe that because wars are still with us,

Below: A false Messiah. Shabbetai Zevi was a 17th century Jew from the city of Smyrna, who claimed to be the Messiah. Many Jews believed him, and this picture shows him entering a city at the head of a delighted procession.

Left: Good and evil. A Russian rabbi, says an old story, was once torn between his good and evil inclinations. "Get up and go to the synagogue!" urged his good inclination. "You must praise God." But his bad inclination had more comfortable ideas. "Stay in bed," it said. "You'll catch cold in this dreadful weather—maybe you'll even die. Don't go out!"

The rabbi hesitated for a little, and then he turned to his bad inclination. "It's kind of you to think of my health," he replied. "I'm worried about your health, too. So *you* stay in bed, and *I'll* go to the synagogue!"

the Messiah has not yet come.

The Messiah is expected to bring complete and lasting peace for all people and nations. One Jewish story shows just how wide the effects of his power would be. A man rushed to the house of the town's rabbi, with the message that the Messiah had come. The rabbi looked out of his window, and saw a dog chasing a cat. "No," he replied quietly, "the Messiah has not yet arrived. The peace he brings will even extend to the animal kingdom."

Some Jews prefer to speak of the Messianic Age, rather than of the coming of an individual. In the Messianic Age people of goodwill everywhere will help in bringing peace.

The afterlife

In common with most religions, Judaism teaches that death is not the end. There is a future eternal existence: a world to come. But precise details about what life will be like in such a world are not part of Jewish belief. Judaism prefers to concentrate on giving life on earth as much meaning and importance as possible.

Left: This picture, from a 16th century manuscript, shows birds' faces instead of human ones. The artist may have been worried about showing human faces because of the Jewish law against making images.

Judaism's many faces

Right: Hassidic Jews follow all aspects of their religion very strictly. The men's fur hats, long side-locks and knee-length coats are part of their customs. This man and his son are praying at the Western Wall.

Right: Samaritans follow many of the laws of the ancient Jews, which modern Judaism no longer observes. They still sacrifice lambs at Passover, just as Jews used to do in their Temple. The Samaritans gather each year for the Passover at Mt Gerizem, on the west bank of the Jordan river.

Right: Women rabbis are accepted only within the Progressive tradition of modern Judaism. This is Rabbi Neuberger, one of Britain's first women rabbis.

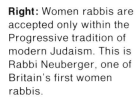

Orthodox and Progressive

Most of the world's Jews can be divided into two groups: Orthodox and non-Orthodox. Orthodox Jews believe that the *Torah* is the word of God, given directly by God and written down by Moses. It is perfect, and the laws contained in it are eternal. They must still be obeyed without question.

Non-Orthodox Jews believe that, while the *Torah* is certainly the word of God, it is also a human document. Parts of it speak to every generation, but other parts belong to just one time, and are not necessarily relevant in today's world. So they say that some laws are eternal, but others can be abolished or changed—and new customs can also be introduced to help Jews cope with modern problems.

The Progressive tradition

Non-Orthodox Jews are known by various names, depending on the country in which they live. The most common names are Conservative, Liberal, Progressive, Reconstructionist and Reform, but the word Progressive can be used to cover them all.

In many parts of the world the Orthodox tradition is stronger than the Progressive one, but in some countries (such as the United States of America) there are more Progressive synagogues than Orthodox ones.

Differences in worship

Perhaps the most obvious difference between Orthodox and Progressive Judaism is found in the synagogue. In Orthodox synagogues men and women worship separately; the men usually within the central part of the sanctuary and the women within an upstairs gallery, or behind a screen or curtain. Progressive synagogues have mixed seating, and men and women sit together at all times.

The reasons for this difference are found in the history of the religion, for Orthodox Jews claim that since men and women sat apart in the ancient Temple, the same positions should be used in the synagogue.

The role of women

Orthodox women are not permitted to play a leading role in synagogue worship, and they are not required to pray as much as men. So their attendance at services is not essential, and the majority of worshippers in Orthodox synagogues will always be men.

Progressive Judaism has always encouraged the full participation of women in religious life. Men and women share equally in the worship. Women may lead the service, preach sermons, and become rabbis.

The language of prayer
Another difference is found in the use of Hebrew. This is regarded as a very important, even sacred, language and Orthodox Jews use it during the whole of their services. They believe that Hebrew is not only a link for Jews with their history, but is also a vital bond between Jews today, all over the world. If synagogue services are held in Hebrew, then a Jew from Britain or North America can visit, say, a French or Italian synagogue and feel at home there.

Orthodox Jews believe, too, that if someone does not understand Hebrew the synagogue services can be followed through translations in the local language, printed in the prayer books. They sometimes use their local language for praying at home. But for public prayer, only Hebrew is used.

Progressive Jews use both Hebrew and their local language for prayers. So in Britain, for example, synagogue services are held partly in Hebrew (to maintain the link with other Jews and with the past), and partly in English (so that those who don't know Hebrew can follow the prayers and understand them).

The use of music
Orthodox synagogues do not use musical instruments on Sabbaths, or during festivals. Instead they have a man to lead the chanting and singing, who is called a *hazan*, or cantor. Sometimes there is also an all-male choir.

Progressive synagogues, however, generally use an organ or some other musical instrument. Only some employ a cantor, but there is often a choir of men and women.

Unity rather than uniformity
Whatever the differences, the common ground is what binds all Jews together. The observance of the Sabbath and the festivals; the concept of God; the aim of making Judaism a living and dynamic religion; the love for Israel: these are all distinctive Jewish ideas which religious Jews share, regardless of their differences.

Above: Being Jewish is not just about being religious. It is also an important part of life for many people who may never enter a synagogue, or pray to God. Here, thousands of people have gathered for an Independence Day Rally in Israel. For them, 'Jewishness' may simply be found in their support for a homeland for their people.

The synagogue

No one is certain just when the first synagogue was built. However, there are historical records to show that it was a well-established and popular institution two thousand years ago, in the Middle East.

At first, the synagogue was a meeting-place: that is what the original Greek word means. (The Hebrew term, with the same meaning, is *beit ha-knesset*.) Later the synagogue also became a place of study and prayer—in fact, an institution for the whole Jewish people. It has always been used as a community centre: where leaders met, where the unleavened bread was baked for Passover, and where perhaps a hostel might exist for the use of travelling Jews.

Many Jews today refer to their house of worship as a synagogue, but some prefer the Yiddish word *shul*. In a few countries (such as the United States of America) a popular name is 'temple'.

Architecture
Synagogues are found wherever Jews live, and their size and style will often depend upon local needs. Some will be no larger than a room, but others are able to seat hundreds of worshippers.

Most synagogues will have been built in the nineteenth century, or may be much more modern—but a few very old ones still exist. The synagogue in the city of Worms, in Germany, was first built in 1034. It was destroyed by the Nazis in 1938, but it was rebuilt in 1958 as an exact copy of the original building.

Features
Some features are found in all synagogues, and it is these which make them Jewish places of worship. Central to any synagogue is the Holy Ark, which houses the *Torah* scrolls. The Ark is covered by an embroidered curtain, and above it hangs the Eternal Light. This is always burning, as a reminder that God's presence, the 'light of the world', is in the synagogue even when no service is taking place.

Either on the curtain, or above the Ark, are two tablets with Hebrew letters on them. The letters identify the first words of the Ten Commandments. Other quotations from the Bible are inscribed just above the Ark.

In the centre of the synagogue, facing the Ark, is a raised platform called the *bimah*. It

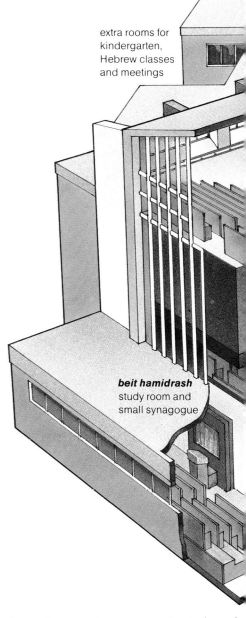

extra rooms for kindergarten, Hebrew classes and meetings

beit hamidrash
study room and small synagogue

is from here that services are conducted, and readings from the Bible made. In some synagogues the *bimah* is directly in front of the Ark.

Many synagogues also have special seats for the rabbi and the cantor—and there is often a row of seats for the wardens. These officials are responsible for the smooth running of services, and work closely with the rabbi and the cantor.

In Orthodox synagogues there is a separate section for women: the one in the picture above has an upstairs gallery.

Functions
Many big synagogues have daily services, both morning and evening, as well as Sabbath and festival services. But because only a few people attend daily prayers, such services are often held in a smaller room.

A modern synagogue is built to house many activities apart from worship. In

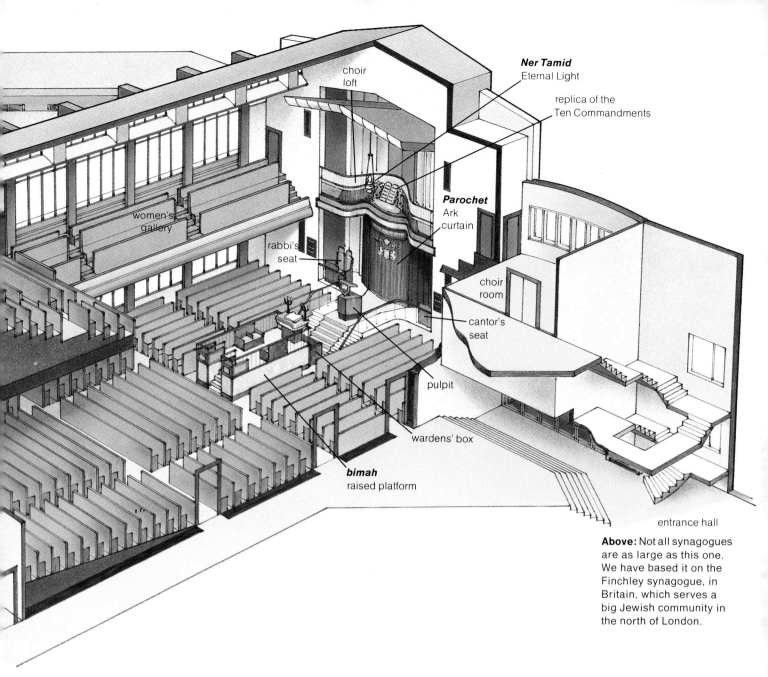

choir
loft

Ner Tamid
Eternal Light

replica of the
Ten Commandments

women's
gallery

rabbi's
seat

Parochet
Ark
curtain

choir
room

cantor's
seat

pulpit

wardens' box

bimah
raised platform

entrance hall

Above: Not all synagogues
are as large as this one.
We have based it on the
Finchley synagogue, in
Britain, which serves a
big Jewish community in
the north of London.

adjoining rooms children learn about their
religion, and attend Hebrew classes. Adult
education programmes are also common.
And there are many occasions for concerts,
lectures, parties and dances.

Large synagogues also have kitchens in
which food can be prepared: from simple
snacks with coffee after a lecture, to three-
course meals for a hundred guests at
weddings or *Bar* and *Bat Mitzvah*
celebrations. This is especially helpful within
Judaism, for its food laws make the choice
and preparation of some foods a very
important matter. The synagogue's *kosher*
kitchens can provide the right sorts of food
efficiently and reliably.

It has been said that the synagogue has
been the most original creation of the Jewish
people, and their greatest practical
achievement. Certainly, for many Jews, the
synagogue is really their second, and
spiritual, home.

Left: This French
synagogue was decorated
in the 18th century. Its
elaborate marble panels
and gilded mouldings are
typical of the time.

You can see that the
synagogue is used by an
Ashkenasi community,
from the way in which
the *Torah* scrolls
are wrapped.

21

A window to heaven

Right: Women are not asked to pray at particular times, nor to wear a skullcap, prayer shawl or *tefillin*. But some women choose to share these traditions with the men, as this young American woman shows by her use of a prayer shawl. The picture on the wall shows the direction of Jerusalem.

The prayerbook

Prayer is important in nearly every religion, and Judaism is no exception. For Jews, prayer is a way of communicating with God. The Jewish prayerbook is called the *siddur*, which means 'order', or 'arrangement'. This word is used because it reflects one important part of the relationship with God: just as God created order in the universe, so Jews create order in their links with their creator.

The *siddur* is one of the great and lasting books of Judaism. It contains many different prayers—of praise, request and comfort.

Praising God

Before asking God for anything, Jewish tradition says that it is polite to praise him. There are many prayers praising God's goodness, power and care. Many of these come from the Bible, especially the Psalms, and begin or end with the Hebrew word *halleluya*, which means 'praise the Lord!'. This prayer is from the Book of Isaiah:
"*Holy, holy, holy is the Lord of hosts,
The whole earth is full of his glory.*"

Most of the first part of a Jewish service is taken up with prayers of praise.

Asking God

A Jewish tradition holds that people can ask God for absolutely anything they want, and he will always answer the prayer. (But people should remember that the reply might be 'no'.) So every Jewish service has special prayers asking God to heal the sick, comfort those in distress or trouble, forgive sins, bring good weather—and for peace:
"*May he who makes peace in the highest
Grant peace to us, and to all Israel.*"

Thanking God

After the requests come the thanks—and many prayers thank God for his care and kindness. In Orthodox synagogues people bow when they say these, to show that they are truly thankful for the gifts of God.

Prayers for special occasions

Short prayers, called *berahot* or blessings, can be said anywhere, and on many occasions during the day. They may be a response to a hundred different events that remind Jews of God's power and goodness: while eating an apple or cake, or when seeing a rainbow, or hearing thunder. This prayer was written to be said when people see a tree blossoming for the first time in spring:
"*Blessed are you, Lord our God, king of the universe, in whose world there is nothing lacking, and who has provided it with good creatures and beautiful trees to give delight to the children of men.*"

Times of prayers

There are three daily prayer sessions: evening, morning and afternoon. Whenever possible the prayers should be said at a public service, but praying at home or somewhere else is just as good. Some prayers, however, may only be said in the presence of a *minyan* (a group of ten men over the age of thirteen).

The form of prayer

In Judaism every public service has a strict order for prayers. One tradition says that everyone should say a hundred blessings each day—and some prayers must be said three times a day, while others must be said twice. But it is not enough just to recite the prayers; they must be said with sincerity.

Special dress

Although there is no Jewish law demanding that men should cover their heads while they pray, it is now an almost universal custom. Any suitable headgear is acceptable, but many wear the *kipah* or *yamelkah* (skullcap). Some Jews keep their heads covered when

they eat, or while they study the sacred books. Very Orthodox Jews keep their heads covered at all times. Most Orthodox synagogues also ask married women to cover their heads.

At morning worship men also wear the *tallit* (prayer shawl). If it is not a Sabbath or a festival day many Jewish men also put on *tefillin*. These are small boxes containing prayers, which are tied to the arm and the forehead. The men in the photograph on page 28 are wearing them.

Movement in prayer
The normal position for prayer is standing, although some less important prayers may be said while sitting down. Originally Jews knelt and bowed in worship as Muslims do, and they still do this in some of the oriental synagogues.

Orthodox Jews bend their knees and bow when certain words are said, and take steps forward or backwards as the prayer suggests. They often sway and swing their bodies, too, as an aid to concentration.

Most prayers are said facing Jerusalem. Many synagogues (and Orthodox homes) have a tablet on one wall, to show the direction in which Jerusalem lies.

A final word
One Hebrew word from the Bible has entered almost every language in the world. It is as common in Christian worship as it is among Jews, and is also used by Muslims. The word is *amen*, and while it is difficult to give an exact translation, it is usually interpreted as 'so it may be', or 'yes, I agree'. It is generally used as a response at the end of prayers.

Above: A synagogue in Tunisia, where the men have gathered for morning prayer and general discussion. They have removed their sandals, in common with their Muslim neighbours' custom.

The sacred books

Far right: The first page of a 14th century copy of the Jewish Bible. The pictures show scenes from the *Torah*. The top row, starting from the right and reading left (as with Hebrew), contains Adam and Eve with the snake; God expelling Adam and Eve from the Garden of Eden; Cain killing Abel; Noah's Ark; Noah pruning his vines after the Flood; and the Tower of Babel.

The word in the middle of the page is the Hebrew word *be-reshit*, which means 'in the beginning'. It is the first word in the Book of Genesis.

The Bible

The oldest sacred book of the Jewish people is the Bible. Christians refer to it as the Old Testament, but Jews usually call it the *Tenach*.

The first five books are considered the most important, and in Hebrew they are called the *Torah*. In English they are sometimes referred to as the Five Books of Moses. It is these books which are found in the *Torah* scrolls, and part of them is read out in the synagogue each Sabbath. Other parts of the Bible are also used for readings, especially some of the Psalms and the Books of the Prophets, but the *Torah* is seen as the revealed word of God. It is the basis of the religion, and the source of its faith.

Rabbinic writings

Another group of holy books was written by the early rabbis, about two thousand years ago. The most important of these is the *Talmud*, which is like a huge encyclopedia, and records the conversations and discussions of many rabbis over hundreds of years. It is a legal code as well as a book of religious customs, and it has moulded Jewish life and thought. It contains references to almost every subject imaginable, including philosophy, science, medicine, industrial

relations and sexual problems. Much of the *Talmud* is written in the form of debates, proverbs and parables, and it even includes funny stories and jokes!

Another work, which contains many stories about Biblical heroes, is the *Midrash*. This tries to fill in gaps in Bible stories, or to explain things that are not clear. One example deals with the Book of Genesis, where there are two different stories about the creation of woman. In Chapter One she is made at the same time as man, but in Chapter Two she is made from the rib of Adam, the first man. The *Midrash* explains this by saying that Adam must have had two wives! The first one, Lillith, was unsatisfactory, and so Adam divorced her. Then he asked God for a second wife, and Eve was created from his own body.

Here are a few examples from the *Talmud* and the *Midrash*:

"*The honour due to parents is like the honour due to God.*"
"*Who is the bravest hero? He who turns an enemy into a friend.*"
"*A man will have to give account on Judgement Day of every good thing he could have enjoyed —and didn't!*"
"*Great is peace! The world cannot conduct itself except with peace.*"

Right: A scribe writing a page of the *Torah*. All copies of the *Torah* are handwritten, never printed.

Signs and symbols

Right: The *mezuzah* contains a piece of parchment, on which the *Shema*, a special prayer, is written. It is attached to the right-hand doorpost of Jewish homes, and is also used on the doors to most rooms inside the house. Some Jews touch and kiss the *mezuzah* as a mark of respect when they enter or leave.

Right: The *menorah* is a special candlestick. This seven-branched kind is the oldest Jewish symbol, and is now used as Israel's official emblem. A nine-branched candlestick is part of the festival of *Hanukah*.

The star of David

In Hebrew this is called the *magen David*: the shield, or star, of David. It is the most widely-used Jewish symbol. The origin of the star is unknown, but it does seem certain that, despite its name, it has no direct connection with the Biblical King David.

It was first used as a symbol in the 17th century by the Jewish community in Prague. The first Zionist Congress in 1897 adopted the star as its emblem, and in 1948 it was included on the flag of the new state of Israel. You can see the star on the back cover of this book.

Food laws

Most Jews, in some way, observe the various food laws. These are based on the Bible's Book of Leviticus, where a long list of permitted and forbidden animals, fish and birds is given.

Only those animals which both chew the cud and are cloven-footed (such as cows and sheep) can be eaten. Pigs, rabbits and horses are forbidden. Fish must have both fins and scales (such as salmon, trout and haddock). Those which do not (such as shellfish and eels) must not be eaten. Birds of prey, such as eagles and partridges, may not be eaten, but those which eat seeds are permitted: chickens and domestic ducks, for example.

Further restrictions

Judaism encourages compassion for animals, and their killing is done in a humane way. It is called *shehitah*, and many non-Jewish experts agree that it reduces the pain felt by the animal to a minimum.

A further ruling states that meat and milk products cannot be eaten together. This means that Jews do not have milk in their drinks or cream on their desserts after a meat meal, and do not use butter on meat sandwiches. Most Jews wait at least three hours after eating meat before they eat a milk product, although the interval varies.

Reasons for the laws

The Bible does not give any reasons for the keeping of these laws. Some Jews think it is healthier; others maintain the laws simply because they think it is a good discipline. But Orthodox Jews believe that God has commanded them not to eat certain foods—and it is their privilege to obey him.

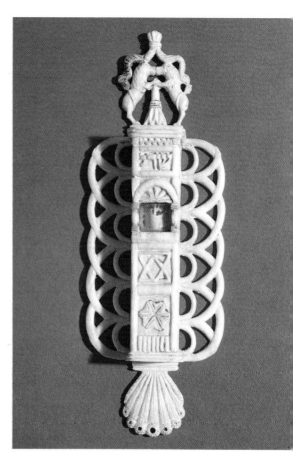

Left: A shop in New York where *kosher* foods are sold. Some shops sell only *kosher* foods, in which the ingredients, preparation and manufacture all agree with the Jewish food laws.

Below: Some of the permitted and forbidden animals are shown here. Permitted foods are called *kosher* in Hebrew; forbidden ones are known as *teraifa*.

eat

Dont eat

Growing up Jewish

Birth

When Jewish children are born they are given both an ordinary name and a Hebrew name. The ordinary name may be chosen from among those which are popular at the time, or it may have Jewish historical meaning —like David or Benjamin, Ruth or Sarah.

The Hebrew name may be given in memory of an important relative: *Moshe* (Moses) and *Rivka* (Rebekah) are two common examples. The Hebrew name is used in the synagogue, and also on religious documents such as wedding certificates.

Circumcision

A boy is given his name during a circumcision ceremony, which is a very important and ancient rite. (Circumcision is important in other religions and cultures too—in fact, one seventh of the world's male population are circumcised, most of them being Muslims.) It is so important that it always takes place on the eighth day after birth, even if that day is a Sabbath. Only illness can delay the ceremony. It is performed by a *mohel*, who is not necessarily a doctor or a rabbi, but is always a specially-trained religious Jew.

Going to school

Most Jewish children attend two schools— their ordinary daytime school with their non-Jewish friends, and a Hebrew or religious school on Sunday mornings and weekday evenings. Part of being Jewish is learning about the religion, so that it will be properly understood.

For some children, the most difficult subject to master is Hebrew. Of course, it is not possible to learn to speak Hebrew fluently just by attending classes for a few hours a week. But the aim is for children to be able to read the Hebrew prayers, so that they can participate in synagogue services.

Other subjects are also taught. The customs and practises of Judaism are very important, and children learn how to take part in these, both in the synagogue and at home. They study parts of the Bible and rabbinic writings, and learn about some of the people who shaped their heritage.

Growing up

Boys must be able to read Hebrew well for their *Bar Mitzvah*, a ceremony which marks a boy's entry into the adult community at the

Right: A *Bar Mitzvah*. The boy is touching the *Torah* scroll with the fringe of his prayer shawl. He will kiss the fringe before he begins to read. *Torah* scrolls are never touched by hand, in case they become dirty or damaged.

age of thirteen. He must be able to chant or read a section from the *Torah* scroll. Some synagogues also expect him to lead the congregation in prayer. At this stage of his life the boy becomes a man, and he is now expected to observe all the Jewish laws.

Girls join the adult community at twelve instead of thirteen, and some synagogues have a similar ceremony for girls, called a *Bat Mitzvah*. In Orthodox synagogues this usually takes place on a Sunday, and seldom on the Sabbath (the day for a *Bar Mitzvah*). Several girls often share a *Bat Mitzvah* ceremony, and they conduct a special service, but they are not allowed to read from the *Torah* scrolls. In Progressive synagogues a *Bat Mitzvah* is exactly like a *Bar Mitzvah*.

The study of Jewish religion and culture does not end with such ceremonies. Many Progressive synagogues hold an additional ceremony for their members at sixteen, and classes continue up to that age. And there are usually youth clubs, often linked to national organisations. These provide opportunities for young people to explore different aspects of their culture.

Left: Reading and writing Hebrew has always been an important part of Jewish education. Jews have always had a very high standard of literacy, even at times in the past when most other people were illiterate.

Below: Hebrew is written and read from right to left. The English translations are shown underneath these quotations, which all come from a book called *Pirke Avot* (Sayings of the Fathers). The vowels are the little marks above and below the lines. Children learn to read and write Hebrew with the marks in, but vowels are often left out in written Hebrew.

עַל שְׁלשָׁה דְבָרִים הָעוֹלָם קַיָם,
עַל הָאֱמֶת וְעַל הַדִּין וְעַל הַשָּׁלוֹם.

The world is preserved by three things : truth, judgement and peace.

אַל תָּדִין אֶת־חֲבֵרְךָ עַד שֶׁתַּגִּיעַ לִמְקוֹמוֹ.

Do not judge your friend until you have been in his place.

אֵיזֶהוּ חָכָם הַלּוֹמֵד מִכָּל אָדָם.

Who is wise? Someone who learns from all people.

The adult years

Marriage

It has always been considered important to marry in Judaism. Although weddings do not have to be performed in synagogues most of them are, but wherever they take place certain things make it clear that the ceremony is a Jewish one.

The bride and groom always stand beneath a *huppah* (canopy), which is often decorated with flowers. The couple drink wine, and promise to uphold the Jewish religion in their new life together. The groom gives the bride a ring, and says a special vow in Hebrew. Then the *ketubah* (marriage certificate) is read and signed by them. Finally, the groom crushes a glass beneath his foot.

No one knows for certain the original reason for this custom. Some say it is done in memory of the destruction of the Temple.

Others say it reminds people that there will always be misfortune as well as prosperity in married life—for the glass is broken while the new couple stand together, just as they will have to do in the future when they face bad as well as good things.

Judaism encourages Jews to marry within the Jewish community. Judaism is mainly centred around the home, and so unless the couple share the same heritage, it is believed, they will be unable to live in total harmony.

It is hoped that every marriage will result in the birth of children, for they are considered very important, and the link between one generation and another.

Divorce

Not every marriage will work, and Judaism recognises divorce, although it is always a matter for regret. Family and friends often rally round to try to save a troubled marriage, and this support may account for the fact that divorce is usually less common in the Jewish community, than in the general community.

In Jewish law a man must give his wife a *get* (divorce certificate) before they can remarry.

Death

Jewish tradition demands that the funeral, and burial, must take place as soon as possible after death—ideally within twenty-four hours, and usually within three days. Funeral services are always very simple, even among wealthy families: only a basic coffin is permitted, and the use of flowers is not encouraged. In death, Jews believe, the rich and poor are equal, and no distinctions should be made between them.

Cremation is not allowed among Orthodox Jews, but it is common in the Progressive groups.

Community life

Synagogues have a number of committees to promote certain activities. These can include parent-teacher associations which raise funds for the Hebrew school, and social committees which organise dances and musical events. Welfare committees ensure that the sick and elderly are visited in their homes, and provided with transport to synagogue functions. Many synagogues also run their own bookshops.

Below: A synagogue wedding. The wedding party is standing beneath the *huppah* (canopy).

As well as such work, many Jews are also involved in outside activities of a general or Jewish nature. Charity and concern for the poor and oppressed have always been important for Jews. Some will raise money for projects in Israel; some will write letters of protest or send parcels for the persecuted Jews of eastern Europe. Others work with the handicapped and elderly in their own community: for example, by providing '*kosher* meals on wheels' for the housebound.

Many Jews are involved in community relations and inter-faith work, which encourages different ethnic and religious groups to meet and talk. Many more work for local and national charities. The Jewish concern for others has come about partly because of their own sad history, and partly because of the commandment in the *Torah*: "You shall love your neighbour as yourself."

Left: Hassidic brides wear heavy veils during the wedding ceremony. The rabbi is holding a container of wine, ready for the couple to sip. You can see lighted candles in the background—another traditional custom.

Below: A Jewish funeral in Brazil. The rabbi is addressing the mourners at the graveside.

A day of delight

The Jewish Sabbath, called *Shabbat* in Hebrew, is a very special day. In the ancient world it was a unique custom, for slaves and servants worked every day, without having time off. Many people thought that a rest day was not necessary.

Tradition links the Sabbath with the creation of the world. According to the story in the Book of Genesis, God made the world in six days, and on the seventh day he rested and was refreshed. So the Jews, who spend six days of the working week at their jobs, should also rest on the seventh day and enjoy the results of their labour.

Today, although the Sabbath is regarded as a day of rest, it is celebrated in three ways: as a day of worship, study and leisure.

Preparation

Although no work is done on the Sabbath itself there is plenty of work to be done in preparation for it, such as shopping, cooking, and preparing the *Shabbat* table. All the food to be eaten is cooked beforehand and kept warm on a low heat or hot-plate in Orthodox homes. Cooking, or lighting the gas, or switching on electricity, is forbidden on the Sabbath day itself. So Friday is a busy day!

The Sabbath begins a little before sunset on Friday night, so in some countries its timing varies from summer to winter, according to the length of the day. In winter it may begin at about three o'clock on Friday afternoon and last for at least twenty-four hours. In summer it may not start before eight in the evening, and end late on Saturday night, making a *Shabbat* of at least twenty-seven hours. Many Progressive Jews, however, begin and end their Sabbath at the same time all year.

Below: The Sabbath candles are lit on Friday evening, a short time before sunset. Custom demands that at least two candles are lit to mark the beginning of the day.

Celebration

Shabbat is welcomed by the woman of the house lighting at least two candles. In some families young girls also light a candle.

In Orthodox homes the men celebrate the start of *Shabbat* in synagogues. In many Progressive homes the whole family go to the synagogue later in the evening, usually after the meal has been completed.

But before eating the meal, all Jews perform a ceremony called *kiddush*. This involves blessing and drinking wine (a symbol of joy), and blessing the day itself. Then the man of the house praises his wife, and blesses his children.

The meal begins with a blessing of bread. There are always two loaves, called *hallot*, made in a special twisted or braided way. During each course *Shabbat* songs are sung, and the meal ends with a thanksgiving.

Activities

The main event is a service at the synagogue the following morning for all the family, followed by a mid-day meal. Many synagogues hold study sessions in the afternoon, although some families study at home. They may also go for walks, or visit friends, or simply rest from the week's work. It is a family day, and ordinary duties are put aside.

The Sabbath ends

The departure of the Sabbath is marked by a ceremony too. Wine is used again, and this time a braided candle with several wicks is lit. A spicebox containing sweet-smelling spices is displayed—and the final act is to pour the wine over the candle to put it out, and for everyone present to wish each other a good week.

Left: A blessing is said over the bread, before the Friday evening meal begins.

Celebrations

Right: The *shofar* is blown on *Rosh ha-Shanah*. It is usually made from a ram's horn, for it was a ram that Abraham sacrificed in place of his son, Isaac. The *shofar*'s curved shape is a reminder that people should bend their will before God. The horn is softened and shaped in hot water, if necessary, to give it the right curve.

It is not always easy to blow the *shofar*, and a lot of practice is often needed. It is usually blown inside the synagogue, but this Jew is sounding the *shofar* at the Western Wall in Jerusalem.

New Year

The Jewish New Year, known as *Rosh ha-Shanah*, occurs in September or October. It is a solemn occasion, for although it celebrates the creation of the world the main emphasis is on judgement. There is a tradition that on this day God opens the 'book of life', in which the names of all people and the deeds they have performed are recorded. During the next ten days (known as the Ten Days of Penitence) God assesses whether or not the bad deeds should be punished with death, and so prayers and repentance are very important.

However, an enjoyable and happy ceremony is held in homes on the eve of the festival. Just before the evening meal pieces of apple are dipped into honey, and eaten by each member of the family. This reminds everyone to hope that the new year will be a sweet and prosperous one.

The Day of Atonement

This is known in Hebrew as *Yom Kippur*, and it is the most solemn day in the Jewish calendar. It happens ten days after *Rosh ha-Shanah*, and it is then that God makes a final judgement, and forgives those who have truly repented. Jews fast for twenty-five hours, and spend most of that time in the synagogue, praying for forgiveness.

Succot

A few days later the Feast of Tabernacles, or *Succot*, is observed. This is a very happy festival, and most families build a *succah* (booth) in their garden. The *succah* is like a hut with no roof, and it is decorated with foliage and fruit. Many families eat their meals in it, and even sleep in it if the weather is fine. In addition, in many synagogues, people build a *succah* for the whole congregation to enjoy. These are all a symbol of trust in God, who protected the Jewish people during their forty years' wandering in the wilderness.

During synagogue services people wave palm branches, myrtle and willow leaves, and a citrus fruit called the *etrog* in all directions, to show that God can be found in all directions and in all lands.

The last day of the festival is really a new holiday, called *Simhat Torah*: the Rejoicing of the *Torah*. It marks the end of the yearly cycle of readings from the *Torah*. All the

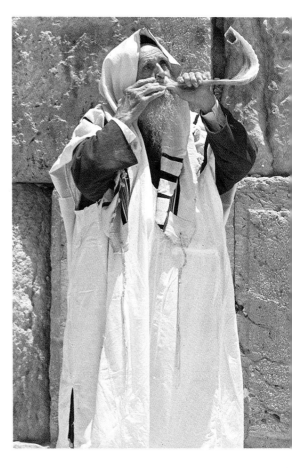

Torah scrolls are removed from the Ark, and processions are made with them around the synagogue. Then the people with the scrolls dance around in celebration. Children often join in too, carrying flags. The last chapters of the Book of Deuteronomy are read out, and followed with the first chapters of the Book of Genesis—showing that God's word never ends, but continues to speak again and again to every generation.

Hanukah

This is also known as the Festival of Lights, and falls in December. It is an historical occasion, for it marks the re-dedication of the second Temple in Jerusalem.

Hanukah lasts for eight days, and each day candles are lit in a special candlestick called a *hanukiyah*, or *menorah*. On the first evening one candle is lit, then two the next night, and so on until all eight are glowing on the final night. (An extra candle is used from which all the others are lit, so in fact the candlestick has nine branches.) Children play a *Hanukah* game with a spinning top, called a *dreidle*, and families eat potato pancakes known as *latkes*.

Left: A kindergarten class prepares for *Hanukah* with pictures of the candlestick.

Left: *Hanukah* is celebrated by the lighting of candles. Most families have a special nine-branched candlestick in their homes, but here a giant outdoor *menorah* forms the backdrop for a *Hanukah* party.

Days of joy

Passover

In late March or early April the most famous of all Jewish festivals is held: *Pesach*, or Passover. This marks the escape of the Jewish people from their slavery in Egypt—and in particular, the night when the angel of death 'passed over' the homes of Jewish children, killing only the children of the Egyptians, as God had promised.

Passover is preceeded by a thorough cleaning of Jewish homes, to remove every crumb of old food. This is because it is the festival of *matzot* (unleavened bread), and the usual bread and rolls will not be eaten for a week. Any other food which may contain yeast is also forbidden.

The *seder*

The most important and popular part of the festival occurs on the first two evenings. It is a home celebration, attended by many members of each family, and friends are also invited. It is known as the *seder*, and during it a special book called the *Haggadah* is read. This tells the story of the exodus from Egypt, and God's delivery of the Jews from slavery to freedom. Many versions of the *Haggadah* have been compiled through the centuries, some with beautiful illustrations. Others have been prepared especially for children—some even with 'pop-up' pictures. Many copies are cherished and handed down from one generation to the next.

The *seder* plate

This contains a number of foods which remind everyone at the table of the festival's meaning:
- A roasted or baked egg; a reminder of the festival sacrifice brought to the Temple in ancient times.
- A roasted lamb bone; which represents the Passover lamb which used to be sacrificed in the Temple.
- Bitter herbs; a reminder of the bitter lives of the slaves in Egypt. Horseradish is often used for this.
- One or two other fresh vegetables (such as lettuce, watercress or cucumber); reminders that this is a spring festival.
- A mixture of chopped apple, nuts, cinnamon and wine; a symbol of the mortar used by the slaves to make bricks in Egypt.
- Finally, a dish of salt water is placed on the table. This represents the tears shed by

the Jews during their long years of captivity.

An extra guest

In this way Jews relive the experience of slavery and freedom, through the eating of these foods and the drinking of wine (everyone drinks four cups of wine). A cup of wine, and a chair, are also provided for the famous prophet Elijah. It is Elijah whose return to the world, it is said, will herald the Messiah's arrival.

An exciting night

The youngest child present at the *seder* will ask the Four Questions from the *Haggadah*, which begin: "Why is this night so different from all other nights?" The rest of the *Haggadah* answers the questions—in stories, riddles and songs. It is certainly a night to remember, for adults and children alike.

Right: The most important ceremony at Passover is the *seder*. All the food and drink on the table has a special meaning, and a particular part to play. You can see the foods grouped on the *seder* plate in the middle. The squares of *matzot* bread are in two piles: at the top of the table, and below the *seder* plate.

Purim

About a month before Passover, another popular festival is observed, although it is not so important as Passover. This is called *Purim*, and the story can be found in the Bible, in the Book of Esther.

Purim is a very exciting time for children. During the synagogue service the story of Esther is read out from a decorated scroll. Every time the villain of the story, Haman, is mentioned all the children make as loud a noise as they can manage. They use football rattles, whistles, pot and dustbin lids—or just hiss and stamp their feet. The idea is to erase Haman's name with sound.

After the service the whole congregation eat *Purim* cakes, called *hamantashen* or *oznei haman*. Children have fancy dress parties, and many people also perform traditional plays called *purimspiel*.

Left: This scroll contains the Book of Esther, from the Bible, which is read out during *Purim*. The scroll is always kept in a case of this shape, called a *megillah*. But the *megillah* is not always made from silver, or so beautifully decorated as this one.

Left: A *Purim* street parade, with fancy dress costumes and elaborately built floats. In Israel, *Purim* is rather like carnival time.

Dreaming of Zion

The homeland of Israel

Jews were exiled from their land for nearly two thousand years, but this did not stop them praying and working for a return. The Passover service has always included a prayer that, next year, the Passover will be celebrated in Jerusalem.

The word 'Zion' is another name for Israel, and in the 19th century a movement grew up amongst Jews that was called Zionism. Many Jews believed that they would never be safe from persecution, or free to practise their religion, unless they returned to Israel. The Nazi slaughter of European Jews in this century convinced many people of the urgent need for a Jewish homeland.

The state of Israel was created in 1948. Since then hundreds of thousands of Jews have emigrated there.

Home of many religions

Most of Israel's citizens are Jews, but 15% of them are non-Jews, and that includes Muslims, Christians, Samaritans, Druse and Ba'hai. Jerusalem, of course, is a very important religious centre for Christians and Muslims as well as Jews, and the city contains many churches and mosques as well as synagogues.

Life on the kibbutz

The *kibbutz* is one of the most famous of Israel's inventions, and it grew from the lives of some of the early Jewish settlers. These people lived together on the land, and developed some of the area's first fruit and vegetable farms. They decided that they would not own anything for themselves, but instead shared everything in common. The money they earned from the sale of their produce went into a common fund, and was used in the ways that everyone agreed were best. Clothes, food, books and work were all shared equally by the whole group.

Today there are about two hundred and fifty *kibbutzim* in Israel, but only about 3% of the population actually live on them (although these include a great variety of people, even university teachers, writers and some government ministers). Not all *kibbutzim* are run in the same way. But the ideas involved in their creation have had an important influence on most aspects of Israeli life.

Conflicts with neighbours

Ever since Jews first began to return to the old land of Palestine, and since the state of Israel was created, there has been serious conflict with the surrounding Arab countries. Palestinian Arabs claim the land of Israel as their own. Tragically, thousands of young people, Jewish and Arab, have died in the wars which have been fought because of disagreements over territory.

Some Jews believed that the state of Israel ought not to be created, for they thought that should wait until the arrival of the Messiah, and the new age of peace and harmony for the world. A few very Orthodox Jews still oppose the existence of Israel. But all Jews, wherever they live, hope to see Israel at peace. They believe that all the countries in the Middle East can benefit, and work together for a shared future.

Right: Celery growing on a *kibbutz*. The women workers are trimming the celery heads before putting them into bags for European supermarkets. Trade in fresh foods is an important part of Israel's economy.

Left: The holy city. Jerusalem has been a place of pilgrimage for thousands of years: first for Jews, and later for Christians and Muslims too. In the foreground is a Russian Orthodox church, and behind it are two mosques.

Left: A street in Tel Aviv, the largest city in Israel and the centre of its business community.

The two men in the foreground show by their clothes that they are religious Jews, but about 80% of the Jews who live in Israel do not practise their religion. The Coca-Cola sign is written in Hebrew; Israel's official language.

The Jewish connection

Far right: This stained glass window was designed by Chagall for Chichester Cathedral, in Britain. Its inspiration comes from two of the Psalms in the Bible, which are about praising God. Everyone, say the Psalms, should be joyful in their praise of God. His name should be praised in dance and song, and with the sound of trumpets, cymbals, timbrels and harps.

You can see the dancing and the musical instruments in the window. King David is near the top, playing his harp.

Right: The Shrine of the Book in Israel, where the Dead Sea Scrolls are kept. These were found in 1947 by a shepherd boy, stored in their original clay pots in a cave near the Dead Sea. The scrolls had survived for 2,000 years! This cylinder displays part of the Book of Isaiah. It is the earliest version in existence.

Judaism's contribution to the world has not only been unique, it has also been an extraordinarily varied one. The most important contribution has been made in religious terms, but Jewish ideas have played a part in almost every aspect of life and thought.

The world's religions
Judaism lives on as a vital religion in itself, but it has also helped to shape two other major religions: Christianity and Islam. Jewish scriptures have become part of the Christian Bible, and both the Christian New Testament and the Muslim *Qur'an* owe much to the work of early rabbis. Many Jewish customs have been adapted by Christians and Muslims, and now form part of their own methods of worship, and festivals.

Hebrew terms, such as Messiah, Sabbath, cherub and jubilee have been adopted by both Christianity and Islam. And Jews and Muslims share many similar beliefs, such as the role of marriage and divorce.

A house of prayer
The synagogue, too, has served as a model for both the church and the mosque. The content of public worship, such as Bible readings and the singing of the Psalms, is similar in synagogues and churches, while the roles of the prayer leaders and the congregations are almost identical in synagogues and mosques.

Concern for life
Judaism has a central concern for the value and importance of life. Some of the early rabbis believed that no human being had the right to kill another—and so, they said, not even a government should kill a murderer. So they opposed capital punishment, centuries before any government abolished the death penalty for murder.

Animal rights
The Jewish concern for life is not restricted to humans, for both the Bible and the *Talmud* contains passages which prohibit the ill-treatment of animals. Today we tend to take such laws for granted, but until the 19th century it was only Jewish law which prohibited cruelty to animals.

Leaders of freedom
Another important Jewish teaching is the future hope of a united human race, at peace. So Jews have often supported the rights of oppressed people, and have been among the leaders of movements which promised freedom. Karl Marx, the founder of communism and one of the most original thinkers of the modern world, was of Jewish origin—and although he rejected all religion, he shared the hopes of the Jewish prophets for a just and equal society.

Prophets of tomorrow
Jews have also been prominent in many other areas of life, from the arts and entertainment to science and medicine. Whether it was building the first 'horseless carriage', introducing sugar and coffee to Europe, or inventing a way of studying the meaning of dreams—the world would be a poorer place without their contributions.

Perhaps the scope of Jewish concerns throughout the ages was prompted by the teachings of prophets such as Micah. His words spoke to Jews thousands of years ago, and their simplicity and directness speak as clearly today. He said:

"He has shown you, O man, what is good, and what does the Lord ask of you but to do justice, and to love righteousness, and to walk humbly before your God?"

Further information

A glossary of useful words

Adonai (Hebrew) our Master. One of the names for God.

amidah (Hebrew) standing. The main daily prayer, which is recited standing up.

atonement an act (or a series of acts) which restores the proper relationship between God and people, after sins have been committed.

cantor a prayer leader in the synagogue, who is trained and chosen for his fine singing voice. Most Jewish communal prayers are sung or chanted to traditional arrangements.

circumcision the removal of the foreskin from the penis in males.

covenant an agreement. Moses (and through him the Jewish people) is said to have received a covenant from God, when in return for God's blessing he promised that his people would keep God's laws.

cremation the burning of bodies after death, instead of burial.

David The most famous King from Biblical times. He lived about 1000 years before the Christian era, and made Jerusalem his capital city. Many of the Psalms are said to have been written by him. The Books of Samuel tell of his life and works.

diaspora a scattering. First used to describe the Jews who were exiled from Israel, but the term now includes all Jews who do not live in the state of Israel.

din (Hebrew) a law.

Elohim (Hebrew) one of the names for God.

Exodus the flight of the Jewish people from slavery in Egypt, led by Moses.

fleishig (Yiddish) meat, or any food that contains meat, or any utensil used to store or cook meat.

Hashem (Hebrew) the Name. Used by Orthodox Jews as a substitute for the word 'God' in ordinary conversation.

Hassidism a Jewish mystical movement which grew from the teachings of Baal Shem Tov in the 18th century. It is an ultra-Orthodox group, but it stresses the importance of prayer, and uses chanting and dancing as aids to communication with God.

Israel the name given by God to Jacob, and so his descendants were called 'the people of Israel'.

kabbalah a mystical tradition which began from thoughts in the *Talmud* about the nature of creation. The most famous kabbalistic book is called *Zohar*, which means 'splendour' in Hebrew.

kashrut (Hebrew) the Jewish food law which states which foods (and especially meat) are permitted or forbidden.

mazal tov (Hebrew) a greeting which means 'good luck'.

milshig (Yiddish) milk, or any food that contains milk, or any utensil used to store or cook milk.

minyan (Hebrew) number. The quorum of 10 men over the age of 13 which is needed for public worship. Most Progressive Jews include women in a *minyan*.

mizrah (Hebrew) east. A tablet which bears this word is often found on the east wall of Orthodox homes, so that worshippers will know which way to face when they pray. In synagogues the Ark is kept in the eastern wall.

Pentateuch (Greek) another name for the Five Books of Moses, or the *Torah*.

phylacteries (Greek) another name for *tefillin*.

psalm a sacred poem or song. The Book of Psalms in the Bible provides much of the material used in Jewish worship.

rabbi (Hebrew) master. A Jewish religious teacher and leader, who is a minister to the community, a leader of synagogue worship, and an interpreter of Jewish law.

sanctuary a holy place. In Judaism this word refers to the main part of the synagogue, where the Ark is kept.

Solomon a King of Israel, and David's son. He built the first Temple in Jerusalem, and for a time made Israel into a powerful state. The first Book of Kings tells of his life and works.

Tenach (Hebrew) the Bible. The word is an abbreviation for the three parts of the Bible: T for *Torah*, N for *Neviim* (the Prophets), and Ch or K for *Ketuvim* (the Writings).

Torah (Hebrew) teachings. This can have three meanings. (1) The Five Books of Moses in the Bible. (2) The Five Books, together with the *Talmud*. (3) The sum total of Jewish thought and learning. It is most commonly used to refer to the first, and it is used that way in this book.

Zion originally this was the name of one of the hills on which Jerusalem was built. It became another name for Israel in the time of the Jewish prophets.

The Jewish calendar

This is based on both lunar (moon) and solar (sun) movements, and was put into its present form about 1,600 years ago.

The months are arranged in pairs. In each pair one month has thirty days, and its partner has twenty-nine days. But because the lunar year and the solar year are different lengths, an extra month has to be added to the calendar seven times every nineteen years. This both keeps the calendar working properly, and the months in harmony with the seasons of the year.

Jewish tradition calculates that the creation of the world took place in 3760BC (or BCE: Before the Christian, or Common, Era). This means, for example, that on 8 September 1983 the Jewish New Year will be 5744. The calculation is in universal use among Jews—but it does not mean that on that day, all Jews believe the world is only 5744 years old!

To see if a particular year is a Jewish leap year (with 13 months rather than 12), divide the Jewish year by 19. If the remainder of the division is 3, 6, 8, 11, 14 or 17—or if there is no remainder at all—it is a leap year. The civil year of 1983–84 is a good example. It is the year 5744 in the Jewish calendar, and when divided by 19 has the remainder 3. So it is a leap year, and will have 13 months instead of 12.

To calculate the Jewish year from a civil year, add 3760 to it. The civil year 1985, for example, is 5745 in the Jewish calendar.

Tishri (Sept-Oct)	Rosh ha-Shanah 1/2 days	Yom Kippur 1 day	Succot 7/8 days	Simhat Torah 1 day
Heshvan (Oct-Nov)				
Kislev (Nov-Dec)	Hanukah 8 days			
Teveth (Dec-Jan)				
Shevat (Jan-Feb)	Tu b'Shvat (New Year for trees) 1 day			
Adar (Feb-March)	Purim 1 day			
Nisan (March-April)	Passover 7/8 days			
Ivar (April-May)	Yom ha'Atzmaut (Israel's Independence Day) 1 day			
Sivan (May-June)	Shavuot 1/2 days			
Tamuz (June-July)				
Av (July-Aug)	Tisha b'Av (Day of Mourning) 1 day			
Ellul (Aug-Sept)				

Left: The Jewish calendar months. They begin with *Tishri*, the month of the Jewish New Year. In leap years, another month of *Adar* is added.

Some of the festivals shown have two numbers for the days during which the festival is celebrated. The smaller numbers are followed by all Jews in Israel, and by many Progressive Jews in the rest of the world.

Books for further reading

A Jewish Family in Britain Vida Barnett (Wheaton 1983)
Visiting a Synagogue Douglas Charing (Lutterworth 1983)
Our Jewish Friends Margaret Clark (National Christian Education Council 1978)
The World of Jewish Faith Myer Domnitz (Longman 1980)
The Diary of Anne Frank Anne Frank (Pan 1983)
The Wonderful Story of the Jews Plantagenet Somerset Fry (Purnell 1970)
When a Jew Celebrates Harry Gersh (Behrman House 1971)
The Way of the Jews Louis Jacobs (Hulton 1972)
The Book of Jewish Holidays Ruth Kozodoy (Behrman House 1981)
My Life Golda Meir (Futura 1976)
The Many Faces of Judaism Gilbert S. Rosenthal (Behrman House 1978)
When a Jew Prays Seymour Rossel (Behrman House 1973)
Judaism Seymour Rossel (Franklin Watts 1976)
The Junior Encyclopedia of Israel Harriet Sirof (Jonathan David 1980)
The Arts and Practises of Living Religions: Judaism Alan Unterman (Ward Lock 1981)

In addition, *The Jewish Year Book* is published each year by The Jewish Chronicle. It gives information about Jewish institutions in Britain, world population figures, and so on. Your local library should have a copy.

Places to visit

Here is a list of national and local art galleries, museums and libraries which have interesting collections of items from the Jewish world. You should always make enquiries before you go to see them, for some items are in reserve collections, or not normally on public display.

Anglo-Jewish Archives (Mocatta Library)
University College, Gower Street, London WC1.

Ben Uri Art Gallery
21 Dean Street, London W1.

The British Museum
Great Russell Street, London WC1.

The Jewish Museum
Woburn House, Upper Woburn Place, London WC1.

Manchester Jewish Museum
190 Cheetham Hill Road, Manchester 4.

National Library of Scotland
Edinburgh 1.

The Parkes Library
University of Southampton, Southampton.

The Porton Library
Leeds 1.

The Sacred Trinity Centre
Chapel Street, Salford.

In addition, your nearest synagogue can be visited. To find out where that is, look in your local Yellow Pages under the 'Religious organisations' entry, or check the Jewish Yearbook (see Books for further reading). You must also check the time of your visit with the synagogue authorities.

Helpful organisations

These organisations all offer help and information. Don't forget to enclose a stamped addressed envelope when you write.

Central Jewish Lecture & Information Committee
Woburn House, Upper Woburn Place, London WC1H 0EP.

Council of Christians & Jews
1 Dennington Park Road, London NW6

Jewish Education Bureau
8 Westcombe Avenue, Leeds LS8 2BS.
A copy of their catalogue is available to teachers, on request.

Israel Government Tourist Office
18 Great Marlborough Street, London W1V 1AF.

Study Centre for Christian-Jewish Relations
17 Chepstow Villas, London W11 3DZ.

Index

Numbers in heavy type refer to picture captions, or to the pictures themselves.

Abraham 10, **34**
Adam 24, **24**
afterlife 17
Africa 14
Akiva 11
Arabic 14
Arabs 8, 38
Arch of Titus **12**
Ark, the Holy **15**, 20, 34
Ashkenasim 14, **15**, **21**
Asian countries 14
atonement 42
Atonement, Day of 34

Babylonians 10
Ba'hai 38
Bar mitzvah 21, 28–29
Bat mitzvah 21, 29
beit ha-knesset 20
berahot (blessings) 22
Bible 10, 20, 22, 23, 24, **24**, 26, 28, 37, **37**, 40
bimah 20, **21**
B'nei Israel 14
Brazil **31**
Britain **18**, 19
Buenos Aires **14**

candlestick **26**, 34, **35**
cantor 19, 20, 42
charities 31
childhood 28–29
choir 19
Christians 10, 12, 14, 16, 23, 38, 40
Christianity 40
church 38, 40
circumcision 28, 42
Cochin **9**
concentration camps 12
Conservative Jews 18
covenant 42
cremation 30, 42

David, King 26, **40**, 42
Dead Sea scrolls **40**
death 30
Deuteronomy, Book of 34
diaspora 42
divorce 24, 30, 40
driedle 34

education 12, 28–29, **29**
Egypt 10, 36
Elijah 14, 36
England 12
   (see also Britain)
Esther, Book of 37, **37**
Eternal Light 20, **21**
Ethiopia 14
Europe 12, 14, **14**, 31
Eve 24, **24**

Exodus 42
Ezra 10–11

Falashas 14
food laws 21, 26, **27**
Five Books of Moses 10, 24
   (see also *Torah*)
France 12, 14
Frank, Anne 12, 44

Genesis, Book of 24, 32, 34
Germans **13**
Germany 14, 20
Greece 14
Greek, the language 20, 42

Haggadah 36
hallot 33
Haman 37
hamantaschen 37
Hanukah 7, **26**, 34, **35**, 43
hanukiyah 34
Hassidic **18**, **31**, 42
hazan 19
   (see also cantor)
Hebrew, the language, 7, 8, **11**, 14, 19, 20, 21, 22, 23, **24**, 26, 28, **29**, 30, 32, 34, 42
Hebrews, the 8
Hillel 11
huppah 30, **30**

Independence Day **19**, 43
India **9**, 14
Inquisition 12
Iran **9**
Isaac 10, **10**, **34**
Isaiah, Book of 22, **40**
Islam 40
   (see also Muslims)
Israel 8, **8**, 10, 12, **14**, 19, **19** 26, 38, 42
Israelis 8, 38–39
Israelites 8

Jacob 8, 10
Jerusalem 6, **9**, **11**, 12, **12**, **14**, 23, **34**, 38, **39**
Judgement Day 24

Kabbalah 42
kashrut 42
ketubah 30
kibbutz 38, **38**
kiddush 33
kipah 22
kosher 21, 27, 31

Ladino 14
latkes 34
Leviticus, Book of 26
Liberal Jews 18
Lights, Festival of 34
   (see also *Hanukah*)
Lillith 24
Los Angeles **14**

marriage 40
   (see also weddings)
Marx, Karl 40
matzot 36, **36**
megillah **37**
menorah **26**, 34
Messiah **16**, 16–17, 36, 38, 40
mezuzah **26**
Micah 40
Middle Ages **13**, 14
Middle East 10, 20, 38
Midrash 24
minyan 22, 42
mizrah 42
mohel 28
Moscow **14**
Moses 10, **11**, 18, 24
mosque 38, 39, 40
music 19, **40**
Muslims 10, 12, 14, 16, **23**, 28, 38, 40

Nazis 12, **13**, 20, 38
New Testament 40
New Year 7, 34, 43
   (see also *Rosh ha-Shanah*)
New York **14**
North America **14**, 19

Orthodox Jews 18–19, 20, 22, 23, 26, 29, 30, 32, 33, 38

Palestine 38
Palestinians 38
Paris **14**
Passover 9, **18**, 20, 36, **36**, 38, 43
Pentateuch 42
persecution 12, **13**, 14, 38
Pesach 36
   (see also Passover)
phylacteries 42
Poland **13**, 14
Portugal 14
Progressive Jews **18**, 18–19, 29, 30, 32, 33
Prophets, Books of 24, 42
Purim 37, 43
purimspiel 37

Qur'an 40

rabbi 17, **17**, **18**, 19, 20, 24, 28, **31**, 42
Reconstructionist Jews 18
Reform Jews 18
repentance 16, 34
Rome 10, **12**
Romans 11, 12
Rosh ha-Shanah 7, 34, 43
Russia 14
   (see also USSR)

Russian Jews **13**, 14
Russian Orthodox church **39**

Sabbath 19, 20, 24, 28, 29, 32–33, 40
Samaritans **18**, 38
sanctuary 18, 42
scribe 24
seder 36, **36**
semitic 8
Sephardim 14–15
shehitah 26
Shema **26**
shofar **34**
shul 20
sidur 22
Simhat Torah 34, 43
skullcap 22
Solomon, King **11**, 42
Spain 12, 14
Star of David 26
succah 6, 34
Succot 6, 34, 43
synagogue **15**, **17**, 18, 20–21, 22, 23, **23**, 28, 29, 30, **30**, 32, 33, 34, 37, 38, 40

Tabernacles, Feast of 34
   (see also *Succot*)
tallit 23
   (see also prayer shawl)
Talmud 24, 40
tefillin 23, **28**
Tel Aviv **14**, **39**
Temple, the first **11**
Temple, the second 6, 11, **11**, 12, **12**, 18, **18**, 30, 36
Ten Days of Penitence 34
Ten Commandments **11**, 20
Tenach 24, 42
Titus, Emperor **12**
Torah 10, 14, **15**, 18, 20, **21**, 24, **24**, **28**, 29, 31, 34, 42
Tunisia **15**, **23**

USA 18, 20
USSR **14**

wardens 21
Warsaw **13**
weddings 21, **30**, **31**, 38
Western Wall 6, **18**, **34**
women 18, **18**, 19, 20, 22, 24, 33

yamelkah 22
Yemen **8**, 14
Yiddish 14, 20
Yom Kippur 34

Zevi, Shabbetai **16**
Zion 38, 42
Zionism 38

Illustration credits
Key to positions of illustrations:
(T) top, (C) centre,
(B) bottom, (R) right,
(L) left.

Artists
Leon Baxter: 17, 27
Tony Payne: 14, 20–1
Rev'd Joshua Sunshine: 29

Photographic sources
© ADAGP Paris 1983/
Sonia Halliday: 41
Bill Aron: 22, 27, 29
Art and Architecture Collection: 12, 21, 35B, 40
BBC Hulton Picture Library: 13TR
Werner Braun: 18C, 19, 34, 37B
Jael Braun: cover, 8, 35T
Stephanie Colasanti: title page, 9, 30
Robert Estall: 38
E.T. Archive/Jewish Museum: 26T
Sally and Richard Greenhill: 36, 39B
Sonia Halliday: 15T
Robert Harding Picture Library: 10, 25
Alan Hutchison Library: 31B
Israel Museum: 17
Jewish Chronicle: 18B
Jewish Education Bureau: 24
Jewish Museum: 37T
Keystone Press Agency: 13B
Nonpareil Publishing Co. Ltd.: 13TL, 16
Bury Peerless: 18T
Rex/Sipa: endpapers, 31T, 32, 33
Scala: 11T
ZEFA: contents page, 8–9, 11B, 15B, 23, 26B, 28, 39T